Examining
Oil and Coal

Jim Levine

SAUNDERS
BOOK COMPANY

Published by Saunders Book Company
27 Stewart Road, Collingwood, ON Canada L9Y 4M7

www.saundersbook.ca

Produced by Red Line Editorial

Library and Archives Canada Cataloguing in Publication

Levine, Jim, author
        Examining oil and coal / Jim Levine.

(Examining Canadian energy)
Includes bibliographical references and index.
Issued in print and electronic formats.
ISBN 978-1-77092-274-7 (bound).--ISBN 978-1-77092-282-2 (pbk.).--
ISBN 978-1-77092-290-7 (html)

        1. Petroleum as fuel--Canada--Juvenile literature. 2. Coal--
Canada--Juvenile literature. I. Title. II. Title: Oil and coal.
III. Series: Examining Canadian energy

TP355.L49 2014   j553.2'820971   C2014-903424-5
                                                   C2014-903425-3

Picture Credits
iStock/Thinkstock, cover, 1, 41; Jaydee Jana/iStockphoto, 5; Dan Barnes/
iStockphoto, 6, 25, 27; Alison Donais/Thinkstock, 8; Ingram Publishing/
Thinkstock, 11; Tiger Gallery/Shutterstock Images, 13; Bigstockphoto, 15; Denis
Roger/Shutterstock Images, 16–17; Juan Camilo Bernal/Shutterstock Images, 19;
Shutterstock Images, 21, 38; Red Line Editorial, 22; Przemek Tokar/Shutterstock
Images, 23; Library of Congress, 29; Vitoriano Jr./Shutterstock Images, 30; Mark
Winfrey/Shutterstock Images, 32; Nathalie Speliers Ufermann/Shutterstock
Images, 33; Peter Close/Shutterstock Images, 36; Steve Jacobs/iStockphoto, 39;
Catherine Yeulet/iStockphoto, 45

Printed in the United States of America
Corporate Graphics Inc.
July 2014

Contents

Energy for the Future

Have your parents complained about the high cost of gasoline? What about the high cost of electricity? People all over the world use a lot of energy. Right now, a lot of the world's energy comes from non-renewable sources. Obtaining and using these non-renewable sources, such as oil and coal, can have negative effects on the environment. And they will eventually run out.

Scientists are constantly looking for ways to improve our sources of energy. Right now, fossil fuels, including oil and coal, make up about 77 percent of Canada's energy needs. Finding ways to make oil and coal more environmentally friendly, less expensive, and last longer are important steps in meeting our future energy needs.

Fossil fuels are the remains of plants and animals that died millions of years ago. These fuels take a very long time to form.

This is what makes them non-renewable energy sources. Fossil fuels include coal, oil, and natural gas. Coal is a black or brown rock made up mostly of carbon. Burning it as fuel releases large amounts of energy. More than half of the coal in Canada is used to generate electricity.

Crude oil, or petroleum, is a liquid fossil fuel. It is made of carbon and hydrogen. Petroleum is converted to gasoline, diesel, and jet fuel, which are our primary sources of energy for transportation. Canada has the world's third-largest oil reserves, after Venezuela and Saudi Arabia. Most of this oil is found in Alberta, Saskatchewan, and the Northwest Territories. About 97 percent of Canada's oil comes from the oil sands in the Athabasca, Peace River, and Cold Lake regions of Alberta and Saskatchewan. Researchers estimate even more oil is available through offshore wells along Canada's east coast.

Gasoline made from oil is a very important part of our modern way of life.

In Alberta, there are more than 100 oil sands projects.

Oil sands are a mixture of sand, clay, water, and bitumen—a type of oil that is too thick to flow freely on its own. Some oil sands are mined using large trucks with shovels. The oil sands are then taken to a facility where hot water is used to separate the bitumen. About 80 percent of oil sands are more than 70 metres underground and are taken from the earth using drilling methods.

Finding ways to mine and use coal and oil more efficiently will play a major role in our energy future.

EXPLORING FOSSIL FUELS

In this book, your job is to learn about how coal and oil are used as energy sources and their role in our energy future. How were these energy sources formed? How are we using them? How do they produce energy? What can we do to make them more efficient and clean?

Noah Carter is travelling to key destinations as part of a field team studying coal and oil. He will meet with experts in the field to help him learn more about oil and coal and how these energy sources fit into our future. Reading his journal will help you with your own research.

Oil Wells

My team and I kick off our research by learning about oil. We've come to an oil well in Sarnia, Ontario. Adam Jacobs, the vice president of the oil company, meets us when we arrive. He explains that oil is a fossil fuel. It formed from tiny sea creatures that lived more than 300 million years ago. When these sea creatures died, they sank to the bottom of ancient oceans and became covered with mud. The layers became thicker until there were hundreds and sometimes thousands of metres of earth covering the dead sea life. Over millions of years, pressure and heat turned the sea life fossils into oil and natural gas.

In 1850, geologist Thomas Sterry Hunt found crude oil in Lambton County, Ontario. A year later, businessman Charles N. Tripp planned to extract the oil from the area. To do this, he created the International Mining and Manufacturing Company. It was the first registered oil company in North America. In 1855, Tripp sold his company to James Miller Williams. Over

Oil well pump jacks like this one were used to extract oil in Lambton County in the 1800s.

the next three years, Williams dug a 15-metre-deep crude oil well. The oil from the well was transported 200 kilometres to a refinery in Hamilton, Ontario. There, it was refined into products such as lamp oil. Later, by the end of the 1880s, more and more cars were produced, and they ran on gasoline. Oil exploration began to boom over the next few decades. By the 1920s, gas stations began popping up everywhere. Since that time, society has become dependent on crude oil.

Mr. Jacobs tells us that the oil well pumps oil from a reservoir underground. "Does anyone know what an oil reservoir is?" he asks. I imagine it's an underground pool of oil, but Mr. Jacobs says this is wrong. He tells us that *petroleum* means "rock oil." Oil reservoirs are actually areas of rock that have droplets of oil stored in the pores, or spaces, of the rocks. There are no underground pools of oil.

We learn that drilling for oil is expensive. Scientists use sound waves to determine the best places to drill for oil. Sound travels through different types of rocks at different speeds. Computers help measure how quickly sound waves move through rock.

"Once we have found an oil reservoir," Mr. Jacobs says, "we drill a production well. As soon as the well hits the reservoir, oil often rises. This is because pressure in the reservoir, from tonnes of rock lying on the oil, is released. As the pressure in an oil well decreases, the oil will no longer rise on its own. Mr. Jacobs tells us that they install pumps at this point to pump the oil out of the ground."

I look at the many pumps around us. I wonder if all oil is pumped on land.

ALBERTA'S OIL BOOM

About 70 percent of the world's oil reserves are found in the Middle East. This region produces more than one-third of the world's oil. In October 1973, when oil companies in the Middle East cut production by 25 percent, oil prices soared. Consumers began to look to other countries to fill the demand. Almost overnight, oil-rich Alberta became the focus of their attention. Throughout the 1970s, more than 4,000 people moved to Alberta each month, and the province's population grew about 30 percent. By the 1980s, more oil was being produced than was needed, so many companies had to decrease production. As a result, the companies needed fewer people to work for them. Alberta's unemployment rate increased significantly, and the once-booming province's economy went into decline. It would be a decade before the province would experience that kind of growth again.

Offshore Drilling

Not all oil is located underneath land. Much of the world's oil is located underneath oceans. To get at this oil, companies need to drill deep into the sea floor. We visit our next destination by helicopter. We land on an offshore oil rig in Atlantic Canada. When we get off the helicopter, a petroleum engineer named Christopher McFarlane meets us. He explains that there are several types of oil rigs, and we are on a semi-submersible rig. These rigs are used in water that is about 70 to 1,000 metres deep.

Drill ships are the next offshore drilling rigs Mr. McFarlane describes to us. He tells us that these rigs are mounted on ships. A drill pipe can be lowered through an opening on the ship's bottom. They can drill in waters up to 3,000 metres deep, so they are useful far from shore. Many of these ships can maintain their position over the well using computerized control systems. Otherwise, the ships can be anchored to the ocean floor.

We get much of our oil from oil platforms built to retrieve oil from deep below the ocean's surface.

After exploratory drilling has shown that a large oil reserve exists, the drilling rig is replaced by a more permanent production platform. These platforms are built to last for decades. Workers even have living quarters on the platforms.

Mr. McFarlane tells us that offshore drilling is a very controversial topic. People who support offshore drilling argue that it will reduce our dependence on oil from other countries and keep gasoline prices lower. There is a lot of oil right off Canada's coasts, and drilling and selling it within the country would be good for the Canadian economy. Other people believe that offshore drilling will ultimately be bad for the country. Continuing to use gasoline will mean increased carbon dioxide emissions into the atmosphere. These people also worry about the environmental impact of offshore drilling. Accidents are rare, but they do happen. And plants and animals suffer when there is an oil spill. These spills can also affect the livelihoods of people who rely on the environment to earn money. If many fish are killed in an oil spill, people in the seafood business will lose money. If oil washes up on beaches, making it unsafe to swim, the hotels and restaurants along those beaches may lose tourists and money as well.

DEEPWATER HORIZON EXPLOSION

On April 20, 2010, the *Deepwater Horizon* offshore oil rig exploded, killing 11 men working on the platform. The rig was drilling an exploratory well in the Gulf of Mexico, about 65 kilometres southeast of the Louisiana coast. The rig burned for 36 hours until it sank into the Gulf on April 22. The 1,500-metre riser pipe connecting the well to the platform broke, causing oil to flow into the Gulf of Mexico. Oil spilled for almost three months until the well was capped on July 12, stopping the flow of oil. About 4.9 million barrels of oil were released into the Gulf, causing billions of dollars in damage. The impact was felt as far north as Canada. Here, the government denied licenses for new offshore drilling operations so it could review environmental regulations.

Oil spills can cause great damage to the environment and the economy.

Wow—I can see why offshore drilling is controversial! We thank Mr. McFarlane for teaching us about offshore drilling. On to our next location!

Turning Oil into Energy

Now that we know how oil is extracted from deep within the earth, my field team wants to know more about how this oil is refined into the fuel that powers our cars and buses. Today my team is visiting an oil refinery in Montreal, Quebec. The refinery is gigantic. There are pipes, tanks, towers, and stacks as far as we can see. I notice something else about the refinery—it smells a little like rotten eggs. "What's that smell?" I ask Irina Kovak, the refinery's senior chemical engineer, who has offered to show us around.

"Crude oil has a lot of different chemicals," she explains. "These need to be removed before the oil can become something useful, like gasoline. The odour you're noticing is the smell of these chemicals being released into the atmosphere. In small amounts, these chemicals won't harm you," she says. "But most refineries are built away from towns and cities for this reason.

It takes a special process to convert oil from the ground into the gasoline that powers our cars.

Still, refineries have to be careful. If a leak or a spill occurs, some of these chemicals can get into the water and be potentially harmful to people and wildlife.

"Crude oil is not very useful when it first comes out of the ground," Ms. Kovak continues. "It is made of many different hydrocarbons. These are chains of carbon and hydrogen atoms. The purpose of the refinery is to separate crude oil into its different parts. Each part forms a different product and has different properties. This is because different hydrocarbons have different numbers of carbons and different arrangements of their chains."

Ms. Kovak explains that the first process occurring at the refinery is this separation. Each of the hydrocarbons present in

Refining crude oil requires a lot of space and equipment.

the crude oil turns from liquid to gas at a different temperature. This allows separation of the parts making up the crude oil. Usually, Ms. Kovak says, the more carbon atoms present, the higher the boiling point. Through a process called fractional distillation, the parts of the hydrocarbons are separated by their boiling points. The mixed hydrocarbons are heated until they turn into gases. The vapours rise through a long column, cooling as they rise higher. As the different parts cool below their boiling point, they condense. This means they change from gas back to liquid.

The final refining process is treatment. After each of the fractions has been separated from the crude oil, refineries must remove the impurities from them. These impurities include substances such as sulphur, nitrogen, oxygen, water, dissolved metals, and salt. Next the different fractions are mixed to create the desired products.

From the refinery, pipelines are usually used to carry the finished products to storage areas. Trucks load the products from there for delivery to customers at locations such as gas stations.

ELECTRIC CARS

Hybrid vehicles use two power sources, usually gas and electricity. Both hybrid and all-electric vehicles help us use oil and coal more efficiently and in ways that are better for the environment. Electric vehicles can convert about 60 percent of the electrical energy to driving power. Gasoline-powered vehicles only convert about 20 percent of the energy stored in the gasoline to driving power. All-electric vehicles don't give off pollution; however, the power plant that generated the electricity usually gives off carbon emissions.

"The refinement process has improved a lot," Ms. Kovak says. "A hundred years ago, only a small part of the oil could be used for transportation fuel. Today, almost the entire barrel of oil can be used. In the past 50 years, improvements in both fuel and vehicles have allowed us to travel about twice as far on a litre of fuel as we could in 1960."

Electric-powered cars use gasoline more efficiently than gasoline-only cars.

She adds, "Did you know that oil even helps bring food to your table? The trucks that transport food crops across the country run on fuels produced from oil."

I guess oil has its advantages and disadvantages, like any energy source. I thank Ms. Kovak for showing us around. We're ready for our next destination!

Into the Seam

After spending time studying oil, my team has switched gears to focus on another fossil fuel: coal. Canada has about 22 coal mines. Most are above-ground, or surface, mines. In those mines, rocks are removed from the area, and huge equipment called excavators are used to dig coal from the earth. Today, though, we are visiting an underground mine in Cape Breton Island, Nova Scotia. When we arrive, the mine superintendent, Don Williams, tells us the mine is located hundreds of metres under the sea. At mines like this one, to get to the worksite, miners either ride down a slope in a small trolley called a rake, or they ride in an elevator called a cage.

Mr. Williams gives us a bit of background on coal. He tells us that like oil, coal is a fossil fuel. It formed from plants that lived in swampy areas more than 300 million years ago. As the plants died, they were covered with more plants, soil, and water. The plants turned to peat, an organic sediment containing

Like oil, coal is made from ancient organisms compressed over millions of years.

partially decayed stems, roots, bark, and twigs. Over time, the pressure from the upper layers squeezed water from the peat. Heat from within the earth caused the peat to break down. Gases were forced out. The peat changed to coal. This process is called coalification.

"Coal has been around a long time," Mr. Williams explains. "For thousands of years humans have been using it as a fuel source for heating their homes. During the Industrial Revolution in the 1800s, huge improvements were made in technology in England and other parts of the world. Much of this technology relied on coal as a fuel, increasing coal's role as an energy source. During this time, steamboats and locomotives became important forms of transportation. Their boilers were fueled by coal."

Peat   Lignite   Sub-bituminous   Bituminous   Anthracite

TYPES OF COAL

There are four different types, or ranks, of coal. They are lignite, sub-bituminous, bituminous, and anthracite. The different ranks contain different amounts of the element carbon and produce different amounts of heat energy. Lignite is the youngest and lowest ranked coal. It is lighter brown and soft. It has the lowest carbon content and energy potential. Anthracite is the oldest, highest rank of coal. It is dark, hard, and shiny. It has the highest carbon content and energy potential.

Machinery, such as the continuous miner, helps us retrieve coal in a safer way.

Mr. Williams tells us the coal seam is the layer of coal between two layers of rock. A large machine cuts coal from the seam. Mr. Williams tells us this machine is called a continuous miner. On the front of the continuous miner is a drum covered with rows of teeth. The drum rotates quickly, allowing the teeth to scrape coal from the seam. The continuous miner scoops the mined coal and moves it to the back of the machine. From there, it flows into shuttle cars that carry it to conveyor belts. The conveyor belts move the coal up to the surface of the mine where the coal will be processed.

DANGEROUS MINING

Coal mines are built with special safety precautions, but mining can still be dangerous. In the past, mines weren't nearly as safe as they are today. Occasionally the mines caved in, sometimes killing everyone inside. Even though mines are much safer today, mining accidents still happen occasionally. Buildups of gas below ground can lead to explosions. On May 9, 1992, a coal mine explosion at Westray Mine in Plymouth, Nova Scotia, left 26 miners dead.

Mr. Williams says traditionally two types of mining methods have been used on Cape Breton Island. "The first are pillars. In this mine, we use a mining process known as room and pillar mining. The continuous miner cuts rooms into the coal deposit, leaving the pillars as supports. The pillars keep the roof of the mine from collapsing on us. The other method is called longwall. Tunnels are carved out of the entire length of the wall of coal. This method is more modern than room and pillar." Mr. Williams tells us that in longwall mining, the roof and overlying rock collapse into the open space behind the miners.

Mr. Williams suggests we look at how the coal is processed and transported. He tells us coal is crushed, sorted, and washed at the processing plant. This removes a lot of the rock and dirt that can't be burned as fuel. He tells us Cape Breton Island has

Huge ships transport about 80 percent of Canada's coal exports from Western Canadian mines.

a network of rail lines that is used to transport coal. A train can pull up to the loading facility and load up under the hopper, the temporary storage for the coal. Mr. Williams tells us trainloads of coal can be shipped to a utilities company. The coal will be burned to generate electricity at a power plant. Power plants use a lot of coal; bigger plants may need an entire trainload of coal almost every day. That's a lot of coal! We decide to visit a power plant next to see exactly how a plant turns coal into energy.

Coal Energy

For our next stop, my team visits a coal-fired power plant in Alberta to find out how coal is used to make electricity. As soon as we arrive, Stephanie Jackson, the plant manager, meets us. "Many parts of the country are phasing out coal due to its harmful effects on the environment," Ms. Jackson says. "Ontario started phasing out coal in the early 2000s, and other provinces, such as Nova Scotia, are looking to do the same. It's still a big industry in Alberta, though. About 90 percent of Canada's coal is found in the western provinces."

She hands me a small vial containing the coal that the plant uses. This coal isn't shaped like rocks as we had seen at the coal mine. Instead it has been crushed and ground into a fine black powder.

"A power plant has a lot of moving parts," Ms. Jackson tells us. "We feed this coal into a firebox where it mixes with air and burns. The firebox provides heat to a big boiler at the

About 60 percent of Canada's coal is steam coal. It is burned to produce electricity for Canadians.

power plant. We pump water through pipes inside the boiler. As the coal burns in the firebox, it heats the water inside these pipes. Once the water becomes hot enough to boil, it changes into steam. The steam is piped to a turbine, a machine with large blades. The pressure of the moving steam turns the blades located in the turbine. As these blades turn, they spin the turbine shaft."

Ms. Jackson tells us that the turbine shaft is connected to a generator. As the shaft turns, the generator changes the spinning mechanical energy into electricity. This is done through magnets that spin in the generator. The spinning magnets produce an electric current in wire coils.

After completing its work in the turbine, the steam is sent to the basement of the power plant into a condenser. The condenser is a large chamber with tubes of cool water running through it. The steam condenses on the tubes, changing back

THOMAS EDISON'S PEARL STREET GENERATING STATION

Inventor Thomas Edison created a working light bulb in 1879. But in order to use it and sell his idea, he needed a way to deliver electricity to customers. In 1882, Edison oversaw the installation of electric conduits and wiring underneath some of New York City's streets. Six giant dynamos were installed on Pearl Street to light up 2.6 square kilometres of the city. The dynamos, known today as generators, produced electricity. Coal was fed into the plant's boilers to provide steam for the dynamos. Pearl Street Station went into service in 1882 and was one of the earliest power-generating plants. Technology, however, changed. Edison's plant could not meet the newer technology's needs. The plant was dismantled in 1895.

into water. The water can then be reused in the boiler. "Large amounts of water are required for this cooling process," Ms. Jackson adds.

After the steam condenses on the tubes in the condenser, the water inside the tubes is hotter. This hot water is then sent to the cooling towers. Ms. Jackson also explains why we sometimes see white clouds above the cooling tower. She says the low-temperature steam entering the cooling tower comes into contact with cool air, cooling the steam to form water droplets in the air. These water droplets may create the clouds we sometimes see. She says this is the low-temperature steam used inside the turbine. It is not smoke, as many people think.

"Coal-fired power plants are more efficient than many other energy sources, such as solar power, and are relatively inexpensive to operate. Right now, about 17 percent of the country's electricity needs are met through coal power," Ms. Jackson tells us. "Plus, even though coal is a non-renewable source, we have a lot of it and much of it can be mined and sold right here in Canada, which is good for our economy."

She adds, "But as with all energy sources, there are some downsides." For one, Ms. Jackson explains, coal-fired power plants release a lot of carbon

U.S. inventor Thomas Edison was a pioneer in using coal power to create electricity.

dioxide gas. This carbon dioxide can be bad for the environment.

"Most older coal plants are only about 30 percent efficient," Ms. Jackson explains. "Think about it this way—if you were cleaning your room at 100 percent efficiency, it would take you an hour. If you were cleaning it at 1 percent efficiency, it would take you 100 hours. New technology can help make plants more efficient." Ms. Jackson adds, "But adapting older plants to the new technology will be expensive."

Our trip to the power plant has given my team a lot to think about. Ms. Jackson said there is technology that can make a coal-fired power plant more environmentally friendly. We decide to investigate further.

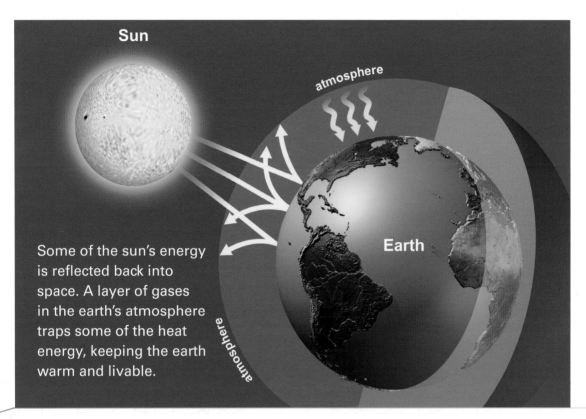

Some of the sun's energy is reflected back into space. A layer of gases in the earth's atmosphere traps some of the heat energy, keeping the earth warm and livable.

GREENHOUSE GASES

When the sun heats the earth, the earth absorbs some of the sun's energy while other energy is reflected to space. A natural layer of gases in the atmosphere traps some of this heat, warming the earth. This is called the greenhouse effect. The gases in the atmosphere are called greenhouse gases. Without the greenhouse effect the earth would be much colder and covered in ice. However, humans are adding greenhouse gases to the atmosphere. Many scientists believe these added gases cause more heat to be trapped on the earth, increasing our planet's average temperature.

Cleaner Coal

After learning about some of the pros and cons of coal power at the Alberta plant, our field team wanted to learn more about the ways to control the air pollution created by burning coal in power plants.

Today, we're staying in Alberta and heading to a coal-fired power plant that has recently constructed a new scrubber, a device that removes pollutants from the gases a coal-fired power plant creates. When we arrive, Greta Weinstein, the power plant's environmental engineer, greets us. She tells us we can call her Greta and invites us to join a training session at the plant to learn how the new scrubber works.

We learn that although carbon dioxide is one of the downsides to coal power, it is not the only pollutant released when coal is turned into energy. Sulphur is a yellow substance found naturally in coal. Some of this sulphur was in the ancient plant life from which the coal formed. Other sulphur came from ancient seawater that had contact with the coal as it

A scrubber is a tall tower that helps a coal-fired power plant control air pollution.

was forming. As coal burns, the sulphur combines with oxygen and forms sulphur dioxide, a poisonous gas that can lead to acid rain.

The Canadian government's clean air regulations limit the amount of sulphur dioxide power plants can release when they burn coal. One way plants can do this is by having a sulphur-removal system in their coal-conversion process if they are burning a high-sulphur coal. One way to remove sulphur is by simply crushing the coal and washing it before burning it. Impurities, such as sulphur compounds, will sink to the bottom, and coal will float during washing.

After combustion, the stage where the coal is burned, the smoke created passes through the scrubber. The plant's cylindrical, tower-shaped scrubber removes sulphur from the power plant's exhaust gases before it is released into the air. Greta says that the process of removing sulphur in the scrubber is called flue gas desulphurization.

I raise my hand. "Is sulphur the only substance that causes air pollution from a power plant?" I ask.

"No, it isn't," Greta answers. "We also remove nitrogen oxides at our power plant."

She explains that nitrogen makes up about 78 percent of the air we breathe. At the high temperatures at which

The sulphur naturally found in coal releases harmful gases when it is burned.

ACID RAIN

Burning fossil fuels can release sulphur dioxide and nitrogen oxides into the atmosphere. When these gases react with water, oxygen, and other chemicals in the atmosphere, mild solutions of sulphuric acid and nitric acid are formed. When these acids fall to Earth as precipitation, in the form of rain, snow, fog, or even dry particles, it is called acidic deposition or, more commonly, acid rain. Acid rain causes lakes and streams to become acidic, a process called acidification. This can harm aquatic life. Acid rain also damages trees. It destroys paint, buildings, statues, monuments, and bridges. Government rules and more awareness of the issue have reduced the amount of acid rain that falls today, but it is still a problem.

coal is burned, nitrogen in air can combine with oxygen to form nitrogen oxides. Nitrogen oxides contribute to respiratory problems, as well as to the formation of smog, a brown haze that hinders visibility.

Greta says that one method for reducing nitrogen oxide emissions uses low-nitrogen oxide burners, which prevent nitrogen oxide from forming in the first place. These burners reduce the amount of oxygen going to the primary combustion area of the burner. With reduced oxygen, the coal does not burn completely. It is then sent to another chamber to repeat a similar process. This occurs until all coal is burned up.

Still, Greta says, it's impossible to make coal completely pollution-free. The scrubbers help remove most of the pollutants, but they can't get them all. Small amounts of pollutants still make their way into the environment.

A Bright Future?

Our last trip is to Saskatchewan, where we're visiting one of the world's first and largest carbon capture storing facilities. The plant's mechanical engineer, Mohammed Assan, meets us as we arrive. He tells us that the plant is partnering with a company in North Dakota to conduct a pilot program using two new technologies. The first is coal gasification. The second is carbon capture.

Mr. Assan tells us that coal gasification is one of the cleanest methods for converting coal into electricity. "The key to coal gasification is a vessel called a gasifier," he explains. "Rather than burning the coal, a gasifier breaks the coal apart using a combination of heat, pressure, and steam. This process produces synthesis gas, known as syngas. Syngas is primarily made up of hydrogen and carbon monoxide and can be burned."

Mr. Assan tells us that next the syngas is cleaned of impurities, such as sulphur and ammonia. Then, it is burned in a two-step power generation process. First, the syngas is burned

Engineers and scientists are working hard to design and build new power plants that are more efficient and better for the environment.

in the combustion turbine. The heat from the combustion turns a generator to produce electricity. Next, the leftover heat from the combustion turbine is used to boil water. This creates steam to turn a steam turbine, also producing electricity. The use of these two types of turbines is called a combined cycle.

"Coal gasification power plants have high power generation efficiencies," Mr. Assan explains. "They also produce less carbon dioxide than traditional coal-fired power plants, so they are cleaner." Mr. Assan tells us gasification has been around for a long time. But as our coal supply keeps getting lower, it will be more important to develop and refine new technologies to make coal use more efficient and make our supply last longer. Right now, gasification plants operate at about 50 percent efficiency. Future gasification plants might approach 80 percent efficiency.

The second technology that Mr. Assan explains to us is carbon capture. He says most power plants burn fossil fuels. This releases large amounts of carbon dioxide into the atmosphere. Carbon capture is a new technology that traps the carbon dioxide from combustion before it is released into the atmosphere. After the carbon dioxide is captured, it is piped deep underground. There, it is permanently stored in rock formations, often more than three kilometres underground.

RECLAIMING COAL MINES

Surface mining of coal disturbs the land. But modern mining practices require mines to be able to be reused, or reclaimed, after the mine is closed. Reclamation restores the land, returning it to a useful purpose. Reclamation involves replacing topsoil that was stripped away. Slopes are evened out. The mining area often becomes a lake or pond. Grass is usually replaced by hydroseeding, spraying a mixture of seed and fertilizer over the ground. Trees are replanted. Reclaiming coal mines also makes the land more attractive to wildlife. Some reclaimed mines can be used as golf courses, fishing areas, or parks.

Most power plants use a steam-powered turbine like this one to create electricity. Gasification adds a second turbine, making the power plants more efficient.

The site is monitored to make sure the carbon dioxide doesn't escape back to the surface. Mr. Assan says that plants using carbon capture also need to make sure carbon dioxide doesn't get into the groundwater people use for drinking.

"Right now, commercial carbon capture plants are very uncommon," he explains. "For one thing, the technology uses a lot of energy and is expensive. If plants were to start using it full time, they would have to raise their prices to pay for it. Your parents' electric bill would probably go up. Still," he adds, "technology will keep improving. New coal plants being built have much stricter regulations than old plants."

If this is true, coal energy will keep getting cleaner. Our team has learned a lot from Mr. Assan. Like oil, coal is an important part of our economy and meeting our energy needs. It is important for us to protect this resource and to make the most of it, while also protecting our environment by finding ways to use coal energy responsibly.

You can help our coal supply last longer by conserving energy. Try replacing your incandescent lightbulbs with LED lightbulbs, which use less energy to light your house.

Your Turn

You've had a chance to follow Noah and his field team as they conducted research on oil and coal. Now it's time to think about what you learned. Coal and oil play a huge role in meeting our current energy needs. They are both fossil fuels that need to be removed from the ground. They can be burned to create heat. This heat can be used directly, such as in a furnace. It can power a turbine to produce electricity. It can also provide transportation energy. Right now, coal and oil are readily available. They will be key energy sources for many years to come.

Coal and oil are also non-renewable resources that will eventually run out. Both create greenhouse gases and other pollutants that can harm the environment. But new methods and technology can help keep these fossil fuels more environmentally friendly and more efficient. More efficient fossil fuels mean our coal and oil supply will last longer. We need to do our best to conserve these non-renewable resources.

YOU DECIDE

1. Do you think the pros of coal and oil power outweigh the cons? Why or why not?

2. Take a look around your house and garage. How many of the objects you see are powered by coal and oil?

3. Think about the advancements being made in coal and oil energy. Which technology discussed has the brighter future? Why?

4. There are positive and negative aspects to all methods of retrieving oil and coal from the earth. Which method do you think is the most positive? Which is the most harmful? Why?

5. What can you do to cut down on your energy use? Think about technology and ways to change your behaviour.

What do you think? Should we try to find ways to use our coal and oil more efficiently? Or should we focus on finding alternative energy sources? Or should we do both?

GLOSSARY

acid rain: The result of sulphur dioxide and nitrogen oxides reacting in the atmosphere with water and returning to Earth as rain, fog, or snow.

barrel: The 159-litre unit used to measure the volume of crude oil.

coal seam: The layer of carbon-rich material located between layers of rock.

coalification: The process that converts plant material into coal due to heat and pressure in the earth.

combustion: A chemical process where something combines with oxygen to burn.

crude oil: Unrefined petroleum (oil).

fossil fuel: A fuel formed in the earth over millions of years from plant and animal remains, including coal, oil, and natural gas deposits.

generator: A machine that converts mechanical energy into electricity.

greenhouse gas: Gas in the atmosphere, such as carbon dioxide or water vapour, which absorbs heat radiated from the earth's surface.

hydrocarbons: Organic chemical compounds composed of carbon and hydrogen.

non-renewable: Something that cannot be replaced by natural environmental cycles as quickly as we're using it.

organic: Material that originated from plants or animals.

petroleum: A thick, yellowish-black, liquid mixture of hydrocarbons.

pores: Open spaces in rocks that can contain air, water, or petroleum.

power plant: A factory that generates electricity.

refinery: A factory that processes and purifies crude oil.

renewable: Something that can be replaced by cycles in nature or the environment.

scrubber: A device that removes impurities or pollutants from a gas.

turbine: A machine that uses a fluid to produce a spinning action. Turbines spin electric generators.

EXPLORE FURTHER

Be a Conservationist

Fossil fuels formed over millions of years. They are a non-renewable resource. Once they're gone, they're gone forever. But, you can conserve fossil fuels by reducing the amount of electricity and petroleum products you use. Turn off lights and televisions when you are not using them. Don't leave doors open for air conditioning or heat to escape. Even recycling aluminum cans saves energy. Look around your home and make a list of ways you can help conserve fossil fuels. Follow this list for a week, taking notes on which of these ways are easy to adapt to and which are hard.

Environmental Emergencies

The Canadian government's Environmental Emergencies Program looks for ways to reduce harmful effects on the environment caused by the release of hazardous substances, such as oil. Various groups across the country work together to create standards and policies for preventing environmental emergencies and taking proper actions should one occur. Visit Environment Canada's website to learn more about different types of environmental emergencies and what to do if one occurs.

Reduce Your Carbon Footprint

The amount of greenhouse gases you produce is sometimes called your carbon footprint. Visit an online carbon footprint calculator to estimate how much carbon dioxide your household produces in a year. Examine your results—where can you reduce emissions? Can you turn off the lights every time you leave a room? Can you replace outdoor electrical lighting with solar-powered lamps? What about growing your own food to reduce driving trips to the grocery store? What are other things you could do to reduce emissions?

How can you help conserve energy?

SELECTED BIBLIOGRAPHY

Bott, Robert D. *Evolution of Canada's Oil and Gas Industry*. The
    Canadian Centre for Energy Information, 2004. Web.
    Accessed March 19, 2014.

"Coal-Fired Power Generation: A Perspective." *National Energy
    Board*. National Energy Board, 2014. Web. Accessed March
    21, 2014.

"Coal Mining." *The Canadian Encyclopedia*. Historic Canada, n.d.
    Web. Accessed March 20, 2014.

ecoEnergy Carbon Capture and Storage Task Force, The.
    "Canada's Fossil Fuel Energy: The Way Forward on Carbon
    Capture and Storage." *Natural Resources Canada*. Canada.
    gc.ca, n.d. Web. Accessed March 20, 2014.

"Men in the Mines." *Nova Scotia Canada*. Province of Nova
    Scotia, 2014. Web. Accessed March 21, 2014.

FURTHER INFORMATION

Books

Horn, Geoffrey M, and Debra Voege. *Coal, Oil, and Natural Gas*. New York: Chelsea Clubhouse, 2010.

Morgan, Sally. *The Pros and Cons of Coal, Gas, and Oil*. New York: Rosen Central, 2008.

Solway, Andrew. *Fossil Fuels*. Pleasantville, NY: Gareth Stevens, 2008.

Websites

http://www.adventuresinenergy.org
Research the processes involved in getting oil and natural gas to the consumer.

http://www.capp.ca
Visit the Canadian Association of Petroleum Producer's site to learn more about where oil comes from in Canada, as well as Canadian oil projects.

http://energyquest.ca.gov/story/index.html
Follow *The Energy Story* to find out all about the energy that makes the world work.

INDEX